STINKIEST!

20 SMELLY ANIMALS

D0469439

STEVE JENKINS

HOUGHTON MIFFLIN HARCOURT · BOSTON · NEW YORK

Stinkiest!

Contents

Whew!

Some animals produce strong smells to mark their territory. They put stinky liquid on branches or rocks to tell other creatures, "This place belongs to me." Animals also use strong odors as a defense. Some of them smell so disgusting that predators leave them alone. And there are a few creatures that smell really bad because of what they eat or what lives in their fur. But what animal is the smelliest of all?

* Words in blue can be found in the glossary on page 38.

Some animals use
strong odors to
defend themselves.

Strong smells can help
an animal protect its
territory.

Smellier than a skunk

The **lesser anteater** lives in the rainforests of South America. It is a good climber and spends most of its time in the trees. When it is in danger, it releases a nasty odor from a gland near the base of its tail. People say that it smells many times stronger than skunk spray.

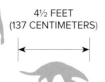

4½ FEET
(137 CENTIMETERS)

The lesser anteater has no teeth—it slurps up insects with a long, sticky tongue.

The lesser anteater is also known as a tamandua. It also defends itself with strong arms and sharp claws.

Where it lives
South America

What it eats
Ants and termites

Stink bomb

The fierce **honey badger** isn't afraid of much. It will even attack a lion or buffalo. But if it does feel threatened, it can defend itself with a stink bomb. A gland near its tail squirts out liquid. It smells so bad that most predators head the other way.

Where it lives
Central and southern Africa, Asia Minor

What it eats
Fruit, seeds, leaves, honey, insects, frogs, lizards, other small animals

The honey badger has tough, thick skin that protects it from bee stings.

3 FEET
(91 CENTIMETERS)

Scaly stinker

The **tree pangolin** hangs from its tail as it eats insects with its long, sticky tongue. Pangolins are the only mammals that are covered in scales. The scales help protect them against predators and the bites of ants and termites. The tree pangolin also defends itself and marks its territory with a stinky fluid.

When danger threatens, pangolins curl into an armored ball. This protects their soft stomach.

Where it lives
Central Africa
What it eats
Ants and termites

15 INCHES
(38 CENTIMETERS)

Tangled up in goo

The **spiny-tailed gecko** lives in the
branches of bushes and trees. If it is in
danger, it squirts a bad-smelling liquid
from its tail. This liquid turns into long,
gooey threads, like a smelly spider web.
These threads stick to an attacker and
give the gecko time to escape.

5½ INCHES
(14 CENTIMETERS)

Some people keep the spiny-tailed gecko as a pet.

Where it lives
Central and northern Australia

What it eats
Ants, crickets, other insects

Urrrp!

European roller chicks have an unusual way of defending themselves. If the young birds are left alone in their nest, snakes, weasels, or other predators may attack them. If that happens, the chicks throw up all over themselves. Their vomit has a strong, unpleasant smell. An attacker usually decides that the baby birds won't be good to eat.

The bad taste and smell of the European roller's vomit comes from toxins in the grasshoppers that the young birds are fed by their parents.

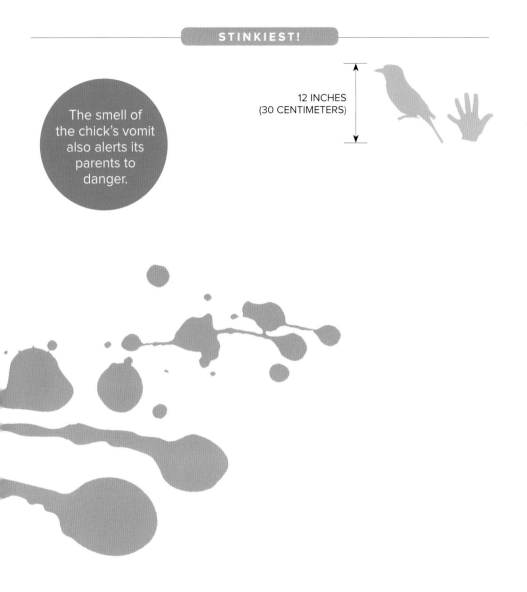

12 INCHES
(30 CENTIMETERS)

The smell of the chick's vomit also alerts its parents to danger.

Where it lives
Europe, western Asia, southern Africa

What it eats (adults)
Insects, frogs, small rodents and reptiles, small birds

Take a step back

The **striped skunk** is a well-known stinky animal. It can shoot a foul-smelling spray into the face of a threatening animal—or human. The spray smells terrible and causes painful burning in an enemy's eyes and mouth.

Where it lives
North America

What it eats
Small mammals, fish, frogs, insects, plants, carrion

The skunk can hit an animal in the face with its spray from more than 6 feet (2 meters) away.

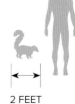

2 FEET
(61 CENTIMETERS)

14

Beetle defense

The **desert stink bug** is a kind of beetle. It has a defense similar to the skunk's. It lowers its head, raises its tail, and sprays a dark, stinky fluid. The unpleasant smell repels most predators.

Where it lives
Western North America

What it eats
Plants, fruit, grains

These insects are also called clown beetles or headstanding beetles.

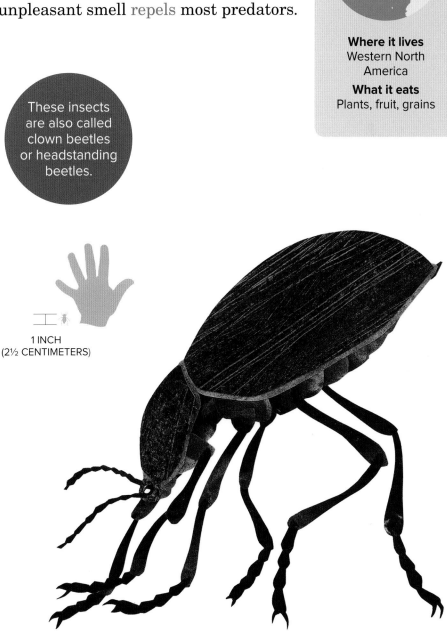

1 INCH
(2½ CENTIMETERS)

Bombs away!

The **bombardier beetle** fires a stream of boiling hot liquid from its rear end to defend itself. It aims this jet at a threatening spider or other animal. The beetle's spray can kill an insect or burn and blind a larger animal.

This beetle's hot spray makes a popping sound when it is fired.

½ INCH
(1¼ CENTIMETERS)

Where it lives
Every continent
except Antarctica

What it eats
Other insects

Two liquids coming
together in the beetle's
abdomen produce this
insect's spray "bomb."

Slinky and stinky

The **king ratsnake** is also known as the "stink snake." If this snake is frightened, it releases a strong odor from a spot near its tail. Humans find this odor disgusting. Animals that might want to eat the snake don't like the smell either.

Where it lives
China, Southeast Asia

What it eats
Rats, rodents, eggs, lizards, other snakes

Even though this snake can smell terrible, many people keep it as a pet.

The king ratsnake is a constrictor. It squeezes its prey to death.

9 FEET
(2¾ METERS)

Don't touch me

If a female **green wood hoopoe** or its nest is attacked, this bird turns its back on the attacker. Then it sprays slimy, stinky oil from an opening near its tail. This oil smells like rotten eggs. It is enough to drive most predators away.

Young hoopoes squirt foul-smelling poop all over their nest it they are disturbed.

15 INCHES
(38 CENTIMETERS)

Where it lives
Central and southern Africa

What it eats
Insects, lizards, fruit, seeds

Stink fight!

Male **ring-tailed lemurs** have scent glands on their wrists and shoulders. These glands produce a smelly liquid that two lemurs will use in a stink fight. The lemurs rub the fluid onto their tails. Then they flick their tails at each other until one of them backs down.

Lemurs also use their scent to say, "Stay away—this territory belongs to me."

Where it lives
Madagascar

What it eats
Plants, fruit, flowers, insects, lizards, birds

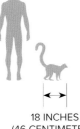

18 INCHES
(46 CENTIMETERS)

Smoke screen

The **sea hare** is a type of sea slug. It lives on the sea floor and protects itself by releasing toxic, bad-tasting purple ink. It also covers itself in a yucky slime.

The sea hare's color varies with the color of the seaweed it feeds on.

A sea hare releasing its ink.

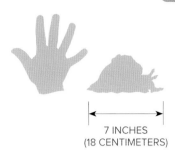

7 INCHES
(18 CENTIMETERS)

Where it lives
Northeastern
Atlantic Ocean,
Mediterranean Sea

What it eats
Seaweed

The sea hare gets its name from the two long "ears" at the front of its body.

Smelly act

The **Virginia opossum** is a talented
actor. If it is attacked, the opossum
plays dead. It rolls over, closes its eyes,
sticks out its tongue, and releases a
foul-smelling liquid from its rear end.
Many predators won't eat dead animals,
so this act can save the opossum.

An opossum that is playing dead can be picked up and moved around without being awakened.

Where it lives
North America

What it eats
Fruit, seeds, worms, insects, snakes, small animals, carrion

The liquid released by an opossum playing dead smells like a decomposing animal

24 INCHES
(61 CENTIMETERS)

25

How does your garden grow?

The **three-toed sloth** lives in the trees of the rainforest. Its fur is often damp, and moss and other plants grow in it. Hundreds of moths and beetles also live in its fur, which has a terrible smell. But this odor does not protect the sloth against the eagles, snakes, and jaguars that hunt it.

Where it lives
Central and South America

What it eats
Leaves, fruit

Sloths are lazy. They spend 16 to 20 hours a day sleeping.

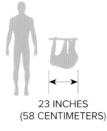

23 INCHES
(58 CENTIMETERS)

The algae and moss growing on the sloth's fur give the animal its greenish tint. This color helps the sloth hide in the treetops.

Bird farts

The **hoatzin** (*hoh-at-sin*) is also known as the "stink bird." It eats leaves that take a long time to digest. The result is a lot of smelly gas—bird farts. Few predators want to eat a bird that smells this bad.

18 INCHES
(46 CENTIMETERS)

Hoatzins spend almost all of their waking hours chewing leaves and plants.

Where it lives
South America

What it eats
Leaves, fruit, flowers

Stinky protection

The **common earwig,** unlike most insects, is a good parent. A mother earwig protects her young before and after they hatch from their eggs. The earwig defends itself and its offspring by squirting a bad-smelling, rancid liquid from openings in the back part of its body.

There is a myth that earwigs like to crawl into people's ears. This is not true.

½ INCH
(1¼ CENTIMETERS)

Where it lives
Worldwide temperate and
tropical areas

What it eats
Insects, plants, algae,
rotting vegetation

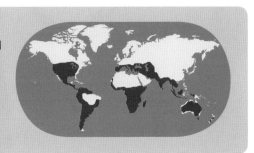

Danger!

For a few weeks each year, a male **African elephant** becomes enraged and violent. It is dangerous to be around. The elephant is going through something called must. When an elephant is in must, a strong-smelling liquid oozes from a gland on its face.

The odor produced by an elephant in must warns other elephants to keep away.

13 FEET
(4 METERS)

A full-grown male elephant is called a bull elephant.

Where it lives
Central and southern Africa

What it eats
Grass, leaves, roots, crops

Bug repellent

Many **millipedes** have a good defense against ants and other enemies. They squirt a foul-smelling and highly toxic spray from openings on their body. One of these millipedes lives in the jungles of South America. Capuchin monkeys rub this millipede on their fur to repel mosquitoes.

Where it lives
Southwest United States, northern Mexico

What it eats
Rotting plant material

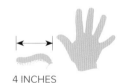

4 INCHES
(10 CENTIMETERS)

Before rubbing it on their fur, the monkeys pop the millipede in their mouth and crush it to release its toxins. This must taste terrible!

Sour spray

The **giant whiptail scorpion** doesn't have a venomous sting. But it does have a powerful defense. It can spray vinegar from a gland near the base of its tail. Vinegar smells and tastes bad, and it stings the eyes and mouth of any predator that gets too close.

Where it lives
Southern United States, Mexico

What it eats
Insects, spiders, millipedes, small frogs

The whiptail scorpion crushes its prey with its powerful claws.

2 INCHES
(5 CENTIMETERS)

Stinkiest of all?

The **striped polecat** may be the worst-smelling animal in the world. It marks its territory with its poop and a powerful-smelling spray. The spray can briefly blind an attacker, giving the polecat time to escape.

Most animals leave the polecat alone—they know how unpleasant a face full of its spray can be.

2 FEET
(61 CENTIMETERS)

The striped polecat
looks like a skunk,
but it is more closely
related to a weasel.

Where it lives
Central and southern
Africa

What it eats
Birds, snakes, frogs,
rodents, insects

Why do some animals smell bad?

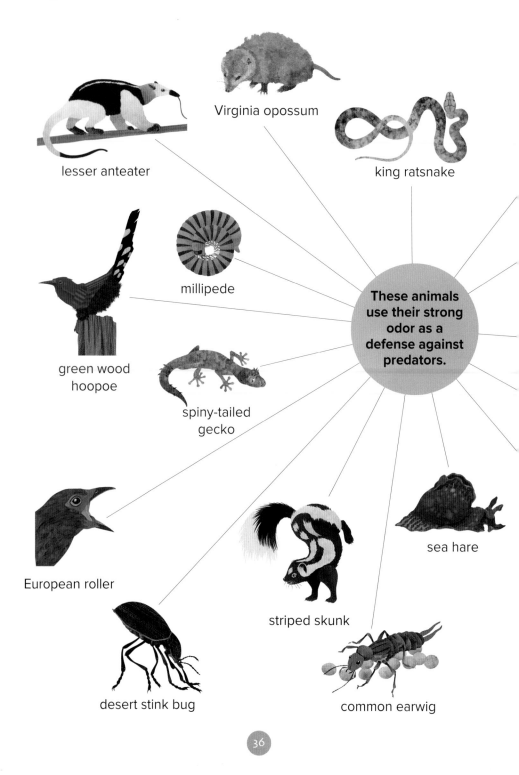

Virginia opossum

lesser anteater

king ratsnake

millipede

green wood hoopoe

spiny-tailed gecko

These animals use their strong odor as a defense against predators.

European roller

sea hare

striped skunk

desert stink bug

common earwig

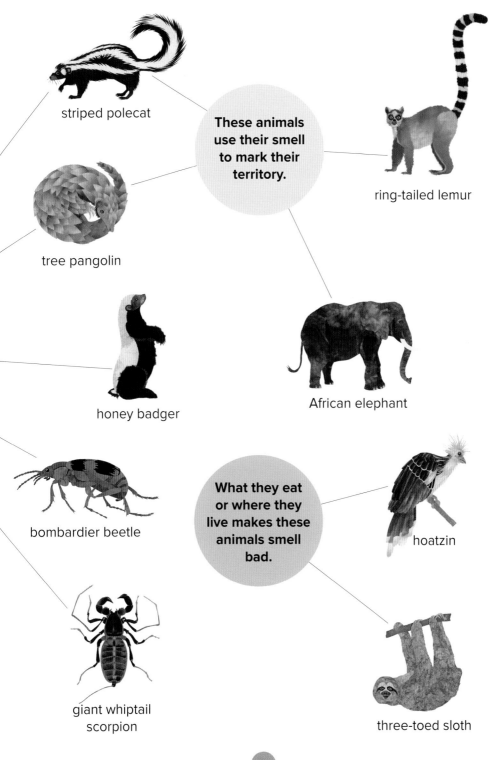

striped polecat

These animals use their smell to mark their territory.

ring-tailed lemur

tree pangolin

honey badger

African elephant

bombardier beetle

What they eat or where they live makes these animals smell bad.

hoatzin

giant whiptail scorpion

three-toed sloth

Glossary

abdomen
Belly or stomach; the back part of an insect or spider.

algae
Simple plants that range in size from tiny single-celled organisms to giant seaweed.

armored
Covered with protective plates or scales.

capuchin monkey
Small monkeys that live in the forests of Central and South America.

carrion
Dead animals.

decomposing
Rotting, decaying.

enraged
Very angry.

fluid
Liquid.

gland
An organ that produces a liquid that serves some function for an animal.

must
Sometimes spelled *musth*. A yearly period in which a mature male elephant becomes aggressive and dangerous.

predator
An animal that kills and eats other animals.

prey
An animal hunted and eaten by a predator.

rancid
A stale, unpleasant taste or odor.

repel
To force or push away.

territory
An area that an animal defends.

toxic
Poisonous.

toxin
A poison produced by a living organism.

vinegar
A sour, strong-smelling liquid.

vomit
To throw up; the contents of the stomach that get thrown up.

Bibliography

Amazing Biofacts. By Susan Goodman. Peter Bedrick Books, 1993.

Animals of the Rainforest. By Stephen Savage. Raintree Steck-Vaughn, 1997.

Elephants. By Alan M. Heatwole. Gallery Books, 1991.

The Encyclopedia of Animals. Edited by Dr. Per Christiansen. Amber Books, 2006.

How Animals Live. By Bernard Stonehouse and Esther Bertram. Scholastic Reference, 2004.

Incredible Bugs. By Rick Imes. Macmillan Canada, 1997.

Infographic Guide to Life, the Universe, and Everything. Thomas Eaton, 2014.

The Life of Mammals. By David Attenborough. Princeton University Press, 2002.

The Most Extreme Animals. By Sherry Gerstein. John Wiley and Sons, 2007.

The Usborne World of Animals. By Susanna Davidson and Mike Unwin. Usborne Publishing, 2005.

The Way Nature Works. Edited by Jill Bailey. Macmillan Publishing Company, 1997.

Wildlife of the World. By DK Publishing. Dorling Kindersley, 2015.

For Robin

hmhco.com

The illustrations in this book were done in torn- and cut-paper collage.
The text type was set in Proxima Nova and New Century Schoolbook.
The display type was set in Geometric.

ISBN: 978-0-544-94478-7 hardcover
ISBN: 978-1-328-84197-1 paperback

Manufactured in China
SCP 10 9 8 7 6 5 4 3 2 1
4500697007

LEXILE: 870
F&P: P